D0436599

THE CHRISTMAS LIST

Library of Congress Cataloging in Publication Number:
2003091888

ISBN: 1-931686-47-5

Printed in Singapore

Typeset in Conduit, Fink, Isabella, Zapf Dingbats

Designed by Bryn Ashburn
Text by Jason Rekulak, Aaron Joslow, and Jennifer Shenk

Distributed in North America by Chronicle Books
85 Second Street
San Francisco, CA 94105

10 9 8 7 6 5 4 3 2 1

Quirk Books
215 Church Street
Philadelphia, PA 19106
www.quirkbooks.com

THE CHRISTMAS LIST

{A Holly, Jolly Treasury of Seasonal Stats}

PHOTOGRAPHY BY DAVID GRAHAM

QUIRK BOOKS

PHILADELPHIA

TO XINA, WHO TAKES CHRISTMAS
VERY SERIOUSLY.

Year of the first Macy's Thanksgiving Day Parade:

1924

Year the Macy's Thanksgiving Day Parade replaced living, snarling lions and bears with harmless inflatable balloons:

1927

Total number of giant balloons in the history of the parade:

167

Number of Macy's employees who participate in the parade:

4,000

Rank of the U.S. government among the world's largest consumers of helium:

1

Rank of the Macy's Thanksgiving Day Parade:

2

{u}

Number of real Christmas trees displayed in the average holiday season:

34,335,809

Number of artificial Christmas trees displayed:

40,694,463

Average number of household fires
caused annually by Christmas trees:

Square acreage of all the Christmas trees growing in the United States:

1,000,000

Square acreage of Rhode Island:

787,800

Age in years of a fully mature Christmas tree:

10

Number of American children hospitalized
in 1997 for ingesting Christmas ornaments:

569

Number of states that feature
a town called "Santa Claus":

8

Number of states that feature
a town called "North Pole":

4

Percentage of Americans who say that Christmas is "too commercialized":

85

Amount in dollars spent by the average consumer on holiday purchases:

1,651

Year in which electric Christmas lights were introduced as a safer alternative to candles:

1895

Percentage of Americans who turn off their Christmas lights on December 26:

Percentage who wait until after January 1:

Number of Americans treated annually for injuries related to holiday lights, decorations, and Christmas trees:

8,700

Odds of a white Christmas in Portland, Maine:

66%

Odds of a white Christmas in Burlington, Vermont:

63%

Odds of a white Christmas in Portland, Maine, prior to the 1990s:

83%

Odds of a white Christmas in Burlington, Vermont, prior to the 1990s:

77%

Percentage of Americans who wear holiday-themed clothing and/or accessories during the Christmas season:

50

Times per minute that Visa cards are swiped in America between Thanksgiving and Christmas:

5,340

Approximate amount in dollars generated by shopping mall photographs with Santa Claus in the United States:

2,255,750,000

{45}

Rank of "Why are there Santas in other malls?" among questions children most frequently ask Santa:

1

Rank of "You never know who the real Santa might be" among the most common answers:

1

Number of Salvation Army kettles throughout the United States:

20,000

Number of hours spent manning the kettles:

4,600,000

Number of days the kettles are in place:

25

Average amount in dollars collected per kettle:

5,625

Percentage of dog and cat owners who have posed their pet in a photograph with Santa Claus:

27

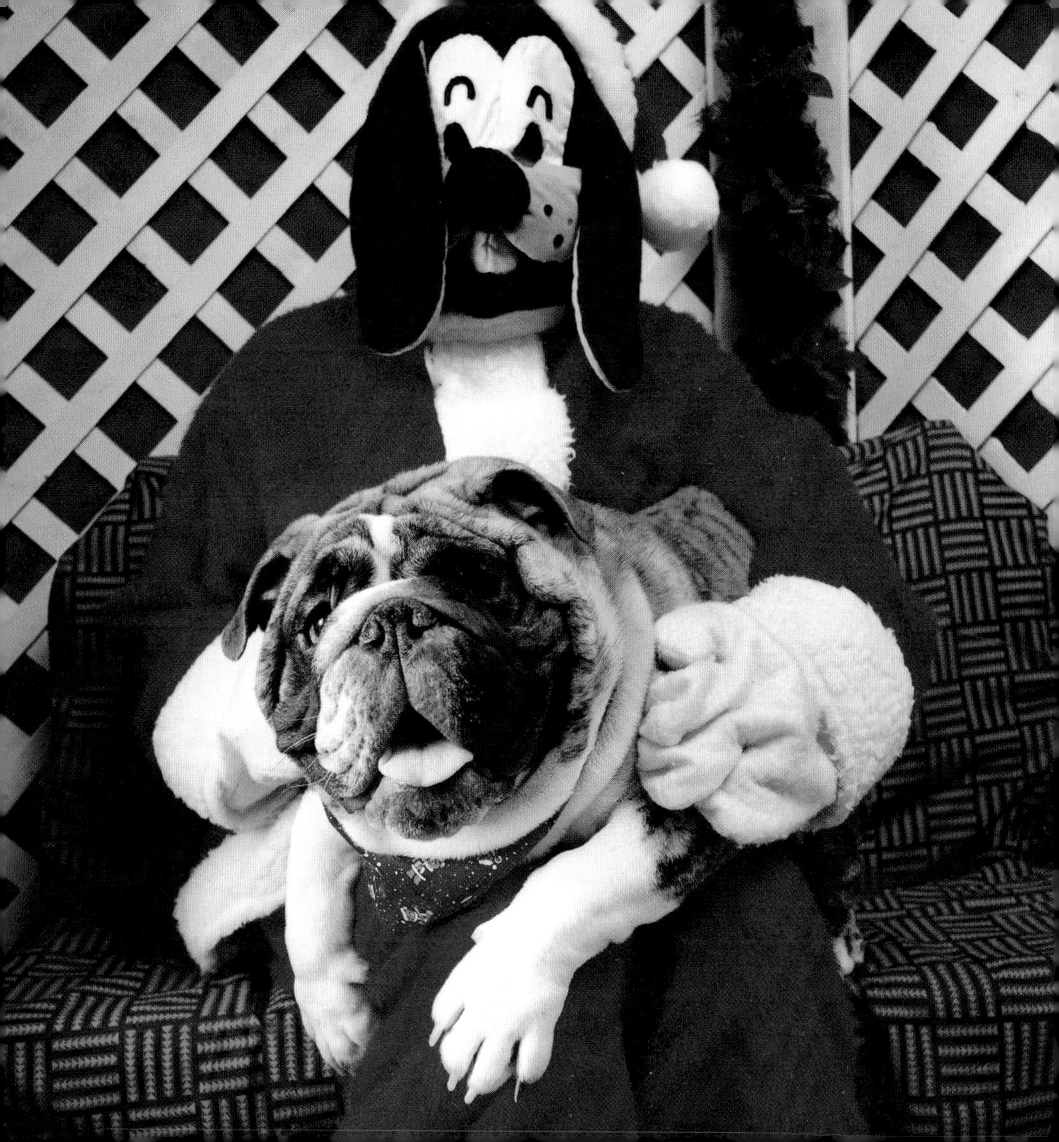

Percentage of Americans who believe Santa drives a sports car during the "off-season":

Percentage who believe he drives an SUV:

25

Number of mall Santa applicants discovered to have criminal backgrounds by Pre-employ.com, an employee screening service:

70

Rank of "Rudolph the Red-Nosed Reindeer" among the most popular Christmas songs of all time:

Rank of "White Christmas":

1

Number of houses Santa must visit on Christmas Eve:

842,000,000

Miles per hour that Santa must travel
to visit all of the world's households
in a single evening:

Percentage of Americans who attend religious services on Christmas:

70

Rank of Americans among citizens of industrialized nations who attend Christmas services:

1

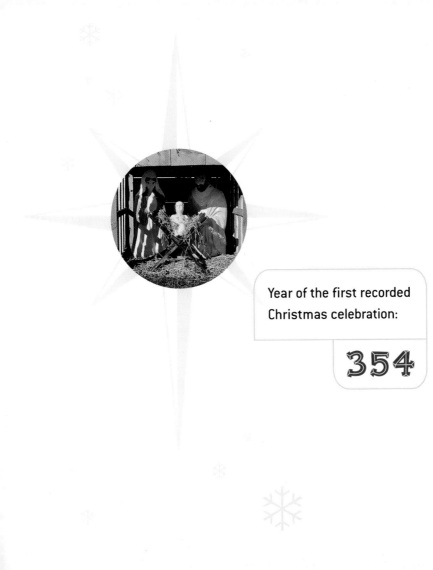

Year of the first recorded
Christmas celebration:

354

Number of times the Bible mentions *three* wise men:

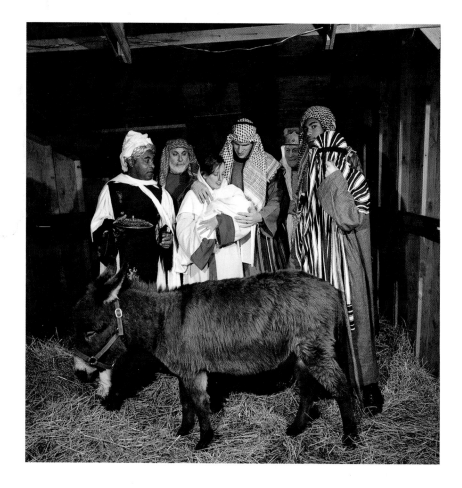

Per capita income in dollars for residents of Bethlehem, Connecticut:

34,017

Per capita income in dollars for residents of Bethlehem, West Bank:

1,030

Rank of *A Christmas Carol* among novels or novellas most frequently adapted for motion pictures:

1

Number of productions to date:

200

Number of soldiers who participated in George Washington's Christmas Eve crossing of the Delaware River:

2,400

Number of spectators who attend annual re-enactments of Washington's crossing:

9,000

Cost in dollars of "The Original Video Fireplace," a ninety-minute videotape of a wood-burning fire complete with "real snap-crackling sounds":

12

Number of Barbie dolls sold every minute around the world:

180

Tons of trash generated annually
by gift wrap and shopping bags:

Percentage of Americans who wait until Christmas Eve to finish their shopping:

Percentage of Americans who admit to "regifting" presents they've received:

Percentage of Americans who make cash or gift donations to charities during the holidays:

71

Number of presents you would have if you received every present described in "The Twelve Days of Christmas":

364

Estimated value in dollars of *The Twelve Days of Christmas*, according to PNC Financial Services:

One partridge in a pear tree:	102.50
Two turtle doves:	58
Three French hens:	15
Four calling birds:	316
Five gold rings:	382.50
Six geese-a-laying:	150

Seven swans-a-swimming:	2,100
Eight maids-a-milking:	41.20
Nine ladies dancing:	4,107.66
Ten lords-a-leaping:	3,921.44
Eleven pipers piping:	1,614.60
Twelve drummers drumming:	1,749.15

14,558.05

SOURCES

pp. 7–8: *Centre Daily Times*; Consumers Union of the United States, Inc.

p. 11: *Centre Daily Times*

pp. 13–15: National Christmas Tree Association

p. 16: U.S. Consumer Product Safety Commission

p. 19: National Christmas Tree Association; The State of Rhode Island; University of Illinois Urban Programs Research Network

p. 20: U.S. Consumer Products Safety Commission; *The Complete Harper's Index Book Volume III* by Charis Conn and Lewis H. Lapham, editors (Franklin Square Press, 2000)

p. 23: Publisher research

p. 24: Gallup Organization; American Express Retail Index, 2002

p. 28: *Christmas in America* by Penne L. Restad (Oxford University Press, 1995)

p. 32: *USA Today*

p. 35: *USA Today*

p. 36: *USA Today*

p. 39: Maritz Marketing Research

p. 40: www.corsinet.com/braincandy

p. 43: U.S. Census Bureau; International Council of Shopping Centers; publisher research

p. 46: General Growth Properties, Inc.

p. 49: The Salvation Army; *The Christian Science Monitor*

p. 50: *American Demographics*

p. 53: Zogby International

p. 54: The Associated Press

p. 57: www.snopes.com/holidays/christmas

pp. 58–61: *The Physics of Christmas* by Roger Highfield (Little, Brown and Company, 1999)

p. 62: Maritz AmericPoll; The University of Michigan Institute for Social Research

p. 65: Microsoft Encarta Encyclopedia

p. 66: Publisher research

p. 69: Connecticut Department of Economic and Community Development; *Christian Science Monitor*

p. 70: *The St. Petersburg Times*

p. 73: WDBJ-TV; *Liberty!: The American Revolution* by Thomas Fleming (Viking, 1997)

p. 74: www.verynicevideos.com

ABOUT THE PHOTOGRAPHER

David Graham's previous books include *Alone Together*, *Taking Liberties*, *Land of the Free*, *Only in America*, *American Beauty*, and *Road Scholar* (with Andrei Codrescu). His photographs can be found in the collections of the Museum of Modern Art (New York), the Philadelphia Museum of Art, the San Francisco Museum of Modern Art, and the Art Institute of Chicago.

He lives in Newtown, Pennsylvania, with his wife and two daughters.